UKRAINIANS

in America

UKRAINIANS

in America

Myron B. Kuropas

Lerner Publications Company • Minneapolis

Front cover: Daria Lysyj, owner of International Gallery and Gifts, with her granddaughter Aleksandra Daria Rieland, in her shop in Minneapolis, Minnesota, June 1994

Page 2: Ukrainian Americans perform their native folk dances throughout the United States.

1996 REVISED EDITION

Library of Congress Cataloging-in-Publication Data

Kuropas, Myron B.
　Ukrainians in America / by Myron B. Kuropas. — 1996
　　rev. ed.
　　p.　cm. — (In America)
　Includes Index.
　ISBN 0-8225-1955-0 (hardcover)
　ISBN 0-8225-1043-X (pbk.)
　1. Ukrainian Americans — Juvenile literature. [1. Ukrainian Americans.]　I. Title.　II. Series: In America (Minneapolis, Minn.)
E184.U5K8　1996
973′.0491791 — dc20　　　　　　　　　　　94-14807

Manufactured in the United States of America

8　9　10　11　12　MP　00　99　98　97　96

CONTENTS

These young Americans preserve their Ukrainian heritage as members of the performing group Arkan.

1
UKRAINE—LAND OF THE TRIDENT

The trident, the symbol of Ukraine

According to the 1990 census, 740,803 Americans of Ukrainian ancestry live in the United States. This figure represents .3 percent of the total U.S. population of 248 million. Although Ukrainian Americans form only a small part of the ethnic diversity of the United States, they have been a visible and productive part of American society.

Those Americans who identify themselves as Ukrainians and who are active in the Ukrainian-American community are concentrated in the metropolitan areas of Philadelphia, Pittsburgh, New York City, northern New Jersey, Los Angeles, Detroit, Cleveland, and Chicago. They support 10 newspapers and more than 50 other periodicals. Ukrainian Americans actively participate in more than 37 organizations that work to preserve the Ukrainian cultural heritage.

Throughout Ukraine's history, its people were repeatedly deprived of independence by their European neighbors. They were often conquered by more than one country at a time. Yet Ukrainians maintained a very strong pride in their heritage. They survived centuries of foreign occupation and geographic division with their identity as Ukrainians still intact. This same ethnic pride works to strengthen Ukrainian Americans' sense of history and community.

The trident, a three-pronged spear, has been the Ukrainian national emblem since early times. A coin dating to the reign of Volodymyr in the 10th century (left) and the trident as it appeared during the days of the Ukrainian National Republic, 1918–1920, (right) are shown here.

Ancient Settlements

Ukrainian history is the story of a valiant people, blessed with one of the most fruitful homelands in the world, who constantly struggled to protect their country from their neighbors. Most of Ukraine's lands are level plains known as steppes. The steppes' fertile, black soil makes Ukraine one of the most productive—and coveted—agricultural regions in Europe.

Ukrainians are ethnic descendants of the Slavs, an agricultural people who occupied the fertile regions north of the Black Sea in eastern Europe for centuries. Sometime in the sixth century, many Slavic tribes began to migrate into areas of central and southeastern Europe. As they settled in different regions, the Slavs intermarried with people already living there. Eventually, the Slavic tribes splintered into different nationalities. Slavic peoples include Russians, Ukrainians, Belarussians, Poles, Slovaks, Czechs, Serbians, Croatians, Slovenes, and Bulgarians. The Ukrainians are one of the largest Slavic nationalities, second only to the Russians. Like other Slavic peoples, Ukrainians have their own language, culture, and history.

When the Slavic tribes arrived in Ukraine, vast areas were uninhabited. The most powerful tribes settled near the Dnieper River and founded the city of Kiev.

In 879 Scandinavian Vikings captured Kiev, and the Slavs became subjects of the Scandinavian royal family of Rurik. Adopting the language, customs, and traditions of the people they conquered, the new rulers developed a powerful state that became known as Rus. In time Rus united all of the Ukrainian-Slavic tribes and built a large, powerful empire known as Kievan Rus.

Planting the Seeds of Democracy

Kievan Rus reached the height of its power in the 10th century. Under the popular Volodymyr the Great, Kievan Rus grew and unified. In 988 Volodymyr adopted Christianity as the state religion and began a massive church and school building program. Eventually, the ancient Ukrainian capital of Kiev became a beautiful city with more than 100 churches and 8 trading centers. At the time of Volodymyr's death in 1015, the Kievan Rus empire stretched from the Black Sea to the Baltic Sea and from the Volga River to the Carpathian Mountains, an area of some 1.2 million square miles.

Yaroslav the Wise, Volodymyr's successor, strengthened Ukrainian Christianity by building churches and monasteries throughout the provinces. Through his efforts, the Eastern Christian Church recognized Kiev as a Metropolitan See, an area overseen by a single archbishop. Yaroslav also wrote the opening section of the Ruska Pravda, the first written code of laws in the Slavic world.

Kiev's St. Sophia Cathedral, a beautiful domed church built in the 11th century

At this time, the people of Kievan Rus had an unusual combination of three forms of government. The prince (the head of the state), the Druzhina (the body of royal landowners), and the Veche (local councils of elected representatives) all shared political control. Since the days of Kievan Rus, the Ukrainian people have cherished democratic self-rule.

After the death of Yaroslav in 1054, Ukrainian history changed course. The Christian Church divided into two separate groups. A western group viewed Rome, Italy, as the center of Christianity. An eastern group believed Constantinople (now Istanbul, Turkey) to be the Christian capital. As religious differences between the two groups increased, each side claimed that the other was not truly Christian. The eastern church came to be called Orthodox while the western church was called Catholic. Since the Ukrainian people inherited their religious tradition from Constantinople during the reign of Volodymyr, they considered themselves part of the Orthodox Church.

Volodymyr the Great

Kievan Rus gradually lost its power. Yaroslav's royal heirs could not agree on a common ruler and fought a series of wars for power. Eventually the house of Rurik split into four separate principalities, or territories ruled by separate princes. What remained of Kievan Rus centered around the principality of Galicia-Volynia in western Ukraine. Disagreements among royal heirs, however, combined with the rising power of neighboring states, eventually led to the fall of Kievan Rus. In the 14th century, Poland conquered Galicia, while Lithuania, then a powerful state north of Ukraine, annexed the province of Volynia and took control of Kiev.

Yaroslav the Wise

A Culture at Risk

The Lithuanians allowed the Ukrainians they ruled to practice and develop Ukrainian customs and institutions. Such good fortune was not to last, however. When Lithuania united with Poland in 1569 to form the Polish-Lithuanian Commonwealth, Galicia, Volynia, and Kiev

In this artist's depiction of Slavic life, a family of serfs shares a one-room dwelling.

Some Ukrainian serfs tended sheep for wealthy landowners.

came under the rule of Polish kings. As subjects of Poland, most Ukrainians became serfs, or farm laborers who served the landowners.

The years under Polish rule were very difficult for Ukrainians. Polish kings, anxious to unite their empire politically, introduced Polonization. This government policy attempted to erase the Ukrainian identity by eliminating Ukrainian institutions and replacing them with Polish ones. By forcing other cultures to conform to the Polish culture, Polish rulers hoped to unite their empire culturally and make their power that much stronger. The Ukrainian Orthodox Church found the Polish policy especially difficult. The Polish government levied extremely heavy taxes on Ukrainian churches. When the churches could not pay these taxes, the government closed them. With no power of their own, and with more and more of their churches closed for tax default, the Ukrainian people's very identity was now at risk.

Ukrainians managed to preserve their national heritage during this trying period in a number of ways. First, groups of Ukrainian priests and their church members, dedicated to continuing Ukrainian traditions, formed Orthodox brotherhoods, or associations. They raised money, printed books, reopened a number of Ukrainian churches, and organized schools. In these schools, young Ukrainians learned the customs and traditions of their ancestors.

Second, the Ukrainian Orthodox Church united with the Catholic Church of Rome in 1596. Pope Clement VIII agreed that the traditional ceremonies and customs of the Ukrainian Orthodox Church would remain unchanged, including the right of priests to marry. In return, this new Ukrainian Catholic Church accepted the pope's authority. Ukrainians hoped that the Polish king, who was also Catholic, would stop his discrimination against their church. But the king continued to meddle in Ukrainian church affairs, prompting some Ukrainian bishops to revoke their earlier acceptance of the Catholic alliance and to return to the Orthodox Church. From that day forward, most Ukrainians have belonged either to the Orthodox or the Catholic Church.

Interior view of St. Nicholas Ukrainian Catholic Cathedral in Chicago

Actor Yul Brynner in a scene from Taras Bulba, *a motion picture about the life of the Cossacks*

Faith and Might—The Cossacks

During the 1500s, a number of adventurous pioneers settled in the uninhabited but richly endowed steppes of eastern Ukraine. These independent soldiers, runaway serfs, and peasants built forts along the Dnieper River to protect themselves from invaders. Although Poland had some control of Ukraine, the Poles were too weak to protect the eastern borders. In these forts (called *sichs),* a military order called the Cossacks was born.

A sich welcomed any male of the Orthodox faith. As each new recruit took his oath of allegiance to the Cossacks, they gave him a new name and told him to forget his past. They permitted neither women nor members of the nobility in the sich and recognized no other authority but that of the *hetman* (commander in chief) or the *ataman* (commander). The Cossacks elected both leaders in a general assembly called a *rada.* They obeyed both hetman and ataman without question during military operations. Their emphasis on equality, military discipline, and democratic rule served to make them members of one of the most unusual societies in all of Europe, as well as a military power. By the mid-16th century, the Cossacks had formed their own state in southern Ukraine, one virtually free of Polish control.

The Cossacks revived the democratic tradition of Ukraine.

In the end, the Cossacks failed to secure a permanent Ukrainian state. The increasingly powerful empire of Russia defeated the Cossacks and took total control of their lands following the Battle of Poltava in 1709. Despite this, the Cossacks contributed immensely to the preservation of the Ukrainian heritage. Fiercely Orthodox, they built churches and supported the Orthodox brotherhoods. Most importantly, they revived the democratic tradition of Kievan Rus and gave the Ukrainian people a period of independence.

After 1709 Russian military and economic power increased rapidly throughout eastern Europe. Poland, weakened from internal strife, fell victim to Prussia, Austria, and Russia. For the next 122 years, Ukraine was ruled by two vast powers, Russia and Austria. Austria (and later Austro-Hungary) controlled Galicia, Bukovina, and Carpatho-Ukraine in western Ukraine and Russia controlled the rest.

Ukraine in the Early 1900s

RUSSIAN EMPIRE

RUSSIAN EMPIRE

GALICIA

CARPATHO-UKRAINE

BUKOVINA

UKRAINE

AUSTRO-HUNGARIAN EMPIRE

Sea of Azov

Border in 1900
Current border

BLACK SEA

The First Ukrainian Americans

The Czechs and Poles, the first Slavic groups to make their way to North American shores, did not begin their immigration until the first half of the 19th century. Not until 1865 did other Slavic groups, among them the Ukrainians, start their move in significant numbers.

Yet historians believe that individual Ukrainians came to North America long before the mass migrations. American historical records from the 17th and 18th centuries contain Ukrainian names. For instance, the English colonist Captain John Smith had traveled in Ukraine and mentioned a Ukrainian man named Lavrenty Bohoon (or Bohun) in his memoirs from that trip. This same man later accompanied Smith to Jamestown, Virginia, in 1607.

American Revolutionary War and Civil War records list a number of Ukrainian names. Also, in 1809 Russia established a fortress and colony near San Francisco, California, called Fort Russ (now known as Fort Ross). Among the early settlers of this colony were Ukrainian Cossacks who had been exiled to Siberia and Alaska by the Russian czars. We know very little about these early immigrants, however.

Reverend Ahapius Honcharenko, a 19th-century American publisher, was born near Kiev in 1832 and graduated from Kiev's Orthodox Theological Seminary, a school for Orthodox priests. When he became the resident chaplain of the Russian embassy in Athens, Greece, he began to speak out against the czar. The Russian secret police arrested Honcharenko, but he escaped to England and continued his verbal and written attacks on the czar.

Honcharenko came to North America in 1865 and settled in San Francisco. On March 1, 1868, he began publishing the *Alaska Herald*, a biweekly newspaper for the people of Alaska and California. With articles in both Russian and English, the *Alaska Herald* helped bridge the cultural gap between the Slavic inhabitants of Alaska and the rest of the United States. The first issue carried the U.S. Constitution in Russian and an English

Ukrainian-born Basil Turchin became a celebrated Civil War general. As a brigade commander for the Union Army, he earned the nickname "The Terrible Cossack" for his daring military attacks.

translation of Ukrainian poetry. A strong supporter of liberty and justice, Honcharenko did not ignore the many injustices in the United States. In one issue, the paper condemned the activities of the Ku Klux Klan, and in another, the paper criticized San Franciscans' mistreatment of the Chinese.

The earliest immigrants from Ukraine were few compared to the large numbers of Western European immigrants. But Ukrainian Americans participated in the settlement of the American colonies and the fight for independence from Great Britain. These immigrants probably wrote to their families, who were struggling against foreign rule in Ukraine, and told of the opportunities available in the United States. Despite the love Ukrainians felt for their homeland, many would soon leave in search of democracy and a better life.

Reverend Honcharenko, surrounded by young American friends, holds a copy of Svoboda, *a supplement to his* Alaska Herald.

2
A NEW LAND BECKONS

During the 18th and 19th centuries in eastern Ukraine, life was as difficult under Russian rule as it had been under Polish rule. The Russian government introduced a policy of Russification and either incorporated Ukrainian institutions into Russian ones or destroyed them. The Russian Orthodox Church absorbed the Ukrainian Orthodox Church in 1686. In

An Easter procession in 19th-century Bukovina, a province of Ukraine

1775 the Russian army destroyed the Zaporozhian Sich, the last remaining Cossack stronghold. In 1781 the Russian empire took over eastern Ukraine, and in 1839 the Russian Orthodox Church absorbed the Ukrainian Catholic Church.

Writing for the People

Despite these measures, the Ukrainian national spirit remained strong and gave rise to a literary revival. In 1798 Ivan Kotlyarevsky published *Eneida,* an adaptation of Virgil's *Aeneid* in which the heroes are Ukrainian Cossacks. This book, the first ever written in the everyday Ukrainian language, gave more Ukrainians literature they could read. Kotlyarevsky's idea sparked a renewed interest in Ukrainian literature.

Taras Shevchenko, a 19th-century poet, achieved great popularity during the Ukrainian literary revival. Born a serf, Shevchenko was considered a man of the people and a genius who captured the true sentiment of the Ukrainian nation and translated it into literature. Severely condemning the Russian czars for their treatment of his people, Shevchenko often referred in his poetry to the freedom enjoyed by Americans. About the American War of Independence, he wrote:

Lesya Ukrainka, a leading writer during Ukraine's literary revival

When will we have a Washington
With a new and righteous law?
One day we shall have him

Shevchenko was arrested for his revolutionary views by the czarist police, forced into military service, and sent to a remote Russian camp where he was forbidden to write. He returned to Ukraine soon after his release, only to die a short time later at the age of 47.

Once Shevchenko's works became widely read, the Ukrainian literary revival could not be stopped. The poet's call for freedom was repeated by many other Ukrainian writers. Afraid that Ukrainians would organize a revolt, the Russian government deliberately stifled the literary revival and any reference to Ukraine's national

Poet Taras Shevchenko (far left) and American stage actor Ira Aldridge became friends when Aldridge visited St. Petersburg as part of a Shakespearean drama troupe.

identity. In 1863 the Russian Minister of the Interior proclaimed that Ukrainians were not a separate nationality, referred to Ukrainians as "Little Russians," and called their language a Russian dialect. Czar Alexander II issued an 1876 proclamation that banned the publication of all books and materials in the Ukrainian language.

In contrast to eastern Ukrainians, western Ukrainians living in the Austrian empire during the 18th and 19th centuries maintained some degree of cultural freedom. The Austrians called Ukrainians living among them "Rusyns" after the ancestral Ukrainian name of Rus. The Austrians allowed the Rusyns to retain their customs and many of their national institutions. The ruling dynasty of Austria gave special consideration to the Ukrainian Catholic Church. For example, Austria allowed Ukrainians to establish seminaries and to create Ukrainian Catholic schools throughout the provinces. Soon a number of educated Ukrainians were trained political leaders of their people.

In 1848 Ukrainians in Lviv established the Rusyn General Council. The council helped create scientific, cultural, and educational societies in Galicia. Scholars delved into Ukraine's long-buried past and produced volumes of valuable research material on Ukraine's distinctive cultural and political history. Other societies throughout Galicia and Bukovina worked to improve the lives of Ukrainian peasants through reading rooms, libraries, choirs, drama troupes, and social clubs. By 1914 hardly a village existed in either province that did not have at least one such organization. In time, many Rusyns in these two provinces began to call themselves Ukrainians.

The province of Transcarpathia (or Carpatho-Ukraine), under Hungarian rule since the 11th century, suffered the most during this period. While the peasants had managed to preserve their heritage and language for hundreds of years, the province's intellectual leaders, especially the priests, had adopted almost all of the Hungarian culture. Once Hungary came under Austrian domination in the early 1700s, the situation improved. A new group of Carpatho-Ukrainian leaders worked to revive their national identity. By 1867, however, Hungary once again controlled Transcarpathia. The Ukrainian national revival there came to a halt.

19th-century writer Ivan Franko urged people in western Ukraine to preserve their heritage and fight for freedom.

A Ukrainian family en route to the United States

Building a New Community—1870 to 1914

During the late 19th century, most Ukrainian immigrants were Rusyn peasant farmers from the provinces of Transcarpathia and Galicia, then under Austro-Hungarian rule. Despite a certain degree of cultural freedom, life for these people was not easy. The average Rusyn had only a small farm and could not afford more land. Ukraine had little industry to provide other jobs. Taxes were high and poverty was widespread. Under these conditions, the average Rusyn could not raise the money to travel to North America. At first only a few could afford to make the trip. They bought passage by selling or renting their land, selling their livestock, and borrowing money from relatives.

Once a few Rusyns made their way to the United States and wrote to their families and friends about opportunities, the first wave of immigration from Austro-Hungarian Ukraine began. Immigration increased so rapidly that at times more than half the population of many villages prepared to leave for North America.

According to immigration records, 67,218 immigrants from Ukraine came to the United States between 1899 and 1906. Another 187,058 arrived between 1907 and 1914. These figures are far from accurate, however. American immigration officials called all people from Ukraine "Ruthenians," the name for Rusyns in English. The immigration officials did not use the term "Ukrainians" as a distinct nationality until 1899. For this reason, a sizable immigration from Ukraine that occurred between 1870 and 1899 was not recorded as such. Even after 1899, many immigration officials, unfamiliar with Ukrainian names, listed some Ukrainians as Poles, Slovaks, Hungarians, or Russians. Some scholars believe that at least 500,000 first- and second-generation Ukrainians lived in the United States by 1914.

Immigrants from Ukraine usually settled where their friends or relatives were already living. Three states—Pennsylvania, New York, and New Jersey—received 85 percent of all Ukrainian immigrants during this period.

Between 1870 and 1914, thousands of Ukrainian immigrants crossed the Atlantic Ocean to America.

Ukrainian-American factory workers lived in Slavic boarding houses such as this one in New York.

Pennsylvania alone attracted 113,204 immigrants from Ukraine, almost half of those arriving. Other states with sizable Rusyn populations in 1914 were Ohio, Illinois, Connecticut, Massachusetts, and Michigan.

In the last half of the 19th century, American jobs were more readily available in industry and commerce than in farming. Western farmland that earlier immigrants had obtained easily was now scarce. Immigrants who were determined to become farmers usually went directly to Canada, which had a large quantity of available land.

Many Rusyn men who immigrated to the United States went to work in the coal mines of northeastern Pennsylvania. They labored long, painful hours, often under brutal conditions. Mine explosions and cave-ins were common. Since no unions existed to bargain for better wages and working conditions, the miner was at the mercy of his employer. Mining companies often lowered wages when they wanted to increase profits. These hardships, combined with the high rate of lung disease among mine workers, made the miner's life difficult.

Rusyns who settled in industrial cities also worked long and difficult hours. These immigrants found jobs in the iron, steel, glass, rubber, shoe, furniture, automobile, and railcar factories, in flour mills, and in sugar refining plants. Although wages were generally lower than miners' wages, working conditions were safer.

Shenandoah, Pennsylvania, was the first organized Ukrainian-American community in the United States. In 1884 America's first Ukrainian Catholic priest, Father

At left is the sod house of a Ukrainian immigrant farmer in North Dakota. Below, breaker boys sort coal from a Shenandoah mine. Many Ukrainians found work in Pennsylvania coal mines.

The first Ukrainian Catholic church in the United States, St. Michael the Archangel (left), was founded by Reverend Ivan Wolansky (right).

Ivan Wolansky, immigrated to the United States. He came from Galicia, where the Ukrainian revival was strong. Wolansky traveled to Philadelphia to present his credentials to Roman Catholic Archbishop Patrick Ryan. But Ryan refused to meet with Wolansky and suggested that, since Wolansky was married, he return to Ukraine as soon as possible. Even though the Roman Catholic Church fully recognized the Ukrainian Catholic Church and its married clergy, Archbishop Ryan would not permit a married priest in his diocese. Wolansky reasoned that only his superior in Lviv could call for his return, and he ignored Archbishop Ryan's suggestion. Wolansky went to Shanandoah and began his work.

By 1885, Wolansky had built the first Ukrainian church in the United States, St. Michael the Archangel, in Shenandoah. He took an extended trip in 1887 from New York to Minneapolis. Along the way, he baptized children, performed marriages, and urged all large Ukrainian settlements to build churches as the first step in organizing their communities.

Wolansky helped organize the Brotherhood of St. Nicholas, the first Ukrainian mutual aid society or "burial society." The society provided money for funeral expenses and loans to its members and their families. In 1886 Wolansky founded *Ameryka*, the first Ukrainian-language newspaper in the United States. He organized a Ukrainian reading room, classes in reading and writing, a choir, and the Cooperative General Store, a self-help enterprise that was owned and managed by Ukrainians. Soon this store had branches in five Pennsylvania towns.

Wolansky was also a union organizer. When a mining strike erupted into violence in 1888, Wolansky, perhaps the only Catholic priest active in the labor movement at the time, helped unify the strikers in their fight against unfair labor practices. His work for Ukrainian Americans ended when the Catholic Church in Ukraine recalled Father Wolansky to Lviv in 1889.

Up until this time, Rusyn immigrants did not refer to themselves as Ukrainians. It was with the arrival of priests such as Father Wolansky that some Rusyns in America began to call themselves Ukrainians. By 1914 only about 40 percent of the immigrants from Ukraine, mostly from Carpatho-Ukraine, called themselves Rusyns. About 20 percent had joined the Russian Orthodox Church in America and referred to themselves as Russians. Through the efforts of Father Wolansky and his successors, the remaining 40 percent adopted "Ukrainian" as their ethnic origin. They identified most closely with Ukraine and its struggle for independence.

The first generation of Ukrainian Americans worked hard to become a vital part of American society and gained national recognition for their efforts. Congress and President Woodrow Wilson proclaimed April 21, 1917, as Ukrainian Day in the United States. On this day, Ukrainian volunteers stood on hundreds of street corners and collected thousands of dollars for aid to Ukraine during World War I.

The first Ukrainian Americans worked hard to become a vital part of American society.

A New Chance for Democracy

While Ukrainian immigrants were forging a new life for themselves in the United States, great changes were taking place in their homeland. The struggle for independence continued for families left behind in Ukraine, and Ukrainian Americans followed these events with concern and hope.

When the Russian revolution of 1917 overthrew the czar, eastern Ukrainians saw a chance for independence. Ukrainian leaders elected a body of lawmakers they called the Rada, the name of the Cossack assembly, to represent all segments of the population.

The Rada introduced many progressive reforms in Ukraine. The Rada abolished capital punishment, released all political prisoners, distributed land to the peasants, and adopted a new constitution that guaranteed the rights of minorities. Ukraine's largest ethnic minorities—the Russians, Poles, and Jews—held three separate cabinet posts in this government. Ukrainian paper currency from this period was probably the only money in the world printed in four languages—Ukrainian, Polish, Russian, and Yiddish.

Shortly afterward, Vladimir Ilyich Lenin and his party of Russian Communists, known as Bolsheviks, overthrew the Russian provisional government. As the new ruler of Russia, Lenin demanded that the Ukrainian Rada give all power to the Bolsheviks, who were then only a minority party in Ukraine. The Rada refused, proclaiming instead the establishment of the Ukrainian National Republic.

Lenin rejected the Rada's proclamation and ordered Russian troops to invade Ukraine. Ukraine's only hope for survival as a free state was to gain recognition of its independence from other countries. So, on January 22, 1918, the Rada declared that from that day forward, the Ukrainian National Republic was "the free, sovereign, and independent state of the Ukrainian people." The Rada then signed a treaty with the Central Powers (Germany, Austro-Hungary, Bulgaria, and the Ottoman Empire) in February 1918. The treaty provided that in return for military assistance, Ukraine would supply the Germans with one million tons of food. With German and Austrian help, the Ukrainian army rid their country of the Russian Bolsheviks. Fighting in Ukraine came to a temporary halt.

The Rada, however, could not deliver the promised food supplies to the Central Powers. Germany overthrew the Rada on April 28 and turned the Ukrainian

Professor Michael Hrushevsky, the first president of the Ukrainian National Republic

government over to a group of landowners who believed in traditional forms of government. They appointed Pavlo Skoropadsky as their hetman, the old title of the Cossack commander. Although he was not popular with most Ukrainians, Skoropadsky was an efficient administrator. He built up the Ukrainian treasury, curbed inflation, and funded the Ukrainian school system.

Several months later, in November of 1918, Germany agreed to stop fighting and end World War I. With that, the Germans withdrew from eastern Ukraine. Supporters of the old Rada regime elected a five-man Directorate, a temporary ruling body, headed by Simon Petlura. Petlura reestablished a democratic Ukrainian republic in eastern Ukraine.

Meanwhile, western Ukraine had also moved toward independence. During World War I, the Austro-Hungarian Empire had collapsed. Groups of Ukrainians, Hungarians, Poles, and Czechs in the fallen empire made plans to declare independent statehood. On November 1, 1918, Ukrainians proclaimed the independence of the Republic of Western Ukraine and indicated their desire to unite with Ukrainians in eastern Ukraine. In an impressive ceremony in Kiev on January 22, 1919, the two republics were formally united into the Ukrainian National Republic.

Despite his best efforts, Simon Petlura could not save the new republic. Three different military forces invaded Ukraine in 1919. Russia's Red Army of the Bolsheviks still wanted a Communist regime in Ukraine and invaded from the east. Russia's White Army of czarists, eager to include Ukraine in a new, non-Communist Russian state, invaded from the south. The Polish army, anxious to add the western provinces of Galicia and Volynia to a new Polish nation, invaded from the west. The Red Army defeated the White Army and signed a treaty with Poland, recognizing Poland's claim to Galicia and Volynia. The Bolsheviks defeated the battered Ukrainian army in 1920 and the Ukrainian National Republic was no more.

From 1919 to 1923, the United States and several European nations signed a series of treaties that again

Pavlo Skoropadsky

Simon Petlura

divided Ukraine. Romania claimed the province of Bukovina. Carpatho-Ukraine, then called Subcarpathian Ruthenia, became a province of Czechoslovakia. In 1922, the newly formed Union of Soviet Socialist Republics (USSR) claimed eastern Ukraine and called it the Ukrainian Soviet Socialist Republic (UkSSR).

During the first years of their rule, the Soviets allowed some cultural and political freedom in the UkSSR. They promised these freedoms to the republics to gain popular support for the Soviet government.

Ukraine Following World War I

BALTIC SEA

USSR

N

Modern Ukrainian border

POLAND

VOLYNIA

• Kiev

CZECHOSLOVAKIA

• Lviv

GALICIA

UKRAINIAN SOVIET SOCIALISTS REPUBLIC

CARPATHO-UKRAINE

BUKOVINA

Sea of Azov

ROMANIA

BLACK SEA

Joseph Stalin, leader of the USSR from 1929 to 1953

The Soviets permitted the Ukrainian Autocephalous (or Independent) Orthodox Church and the Ukrainian Academy of Sciences, both organizations of the Ukrainian National Republic, to continue their work among the Ukrainian people. The use of the Ukrainian language as the only language of instruction strengthened Ukraine's school system. During this period, Ukrainians founded new literary organizations and published many books, newspapers, and other periodicals.

But this cultural progress was reversed soon after Joseph Stalin rose to power in the USSR. Little by little, the new dictator restored the Russification policies of the czars. Between 1929 and 1939, he replaced almost 75 percent of the Communist Party leadership in Ukraine with non-Ukrainians loyal to Moscow. He also replaced Ukrainian scientists, scholars, and educators who resisted Soviet control. Falsely accused of anti-Soviet crimes, most were killed or deported to Siberia. The antireligious Soviets also imprisoned Ukrainian Orthodox Church leaders and placed all Ukrainian churches under the jurisdiction of the Soviet-controlled Russian Orthodox Church.

A political cartoonist depicts the cause of the 1932–1933 famine: confiscation by the Soviet government of every sack of flour.

In 1990, Ukrainian farmers still worked on collectives.

Hardest hit by the Stalin regime were Ukrainian farmers. Not long after Stalin took over the Communist Party, he began a program to make the Soviet Union one of the world's leading industrial powers. To do this, he needed large amounts of cash and decided to get the money by increasing the Soviet Union's agricultural exports. He abolished individually owned farms and turned them into state-run farms, or collectives. If any Ukrainians resisted the program, they were shot or deported to Siberian labor camps. The Soviets demanded that every collective in Ukraine and the other republics contribute a certain percentage of its yearly crop to the USSR. By 1932 Ukraine's contribution had increased to such a high proportion that Ukrainian farmers were left nothing to eat. Armed government agents seized all grain and food. The famine caused by this grain seizure resulted in some seven million Ukrainian deaths in 1932 and 1933.

To further weaken Ukrainian resistance, Stalin deported some four million Ukrainians to other parts of the Soviet Union and sent Russians and other peoples to replace them in the UkSSR.

Ukrainian-American demonstrators commemorate the 50th anniversary of the famine in Ukraine.

33

In the 1920s, many Ukrainian immigrants took the oath to become U.S. citizens.

The Community Grows—1920 to 1939

After World War I, the United States passed a series of new immigration laws that established quotas. These quotas limited the number of people allowed into the United States from a particular country in one year. The U.S. government severely limited the immigration of Ukrainians and other nationalities. As a result, no more than 40,000 Ukrainians came to the United States between the years 1920 and 1939, the period called the second immigration. Those who did immigrate usually came from sections of Ukraine outside the UkSSR, since the Soviet Union permitted few Ukrainians to leave.

During this period, the center of Ukrainian-American community life shifted from the coal regions of Pennsylvania to the large urban areas of the East and Midwest. Six cities—New York, Philadelphia, Pittsburgh, Cleveland, Detroit, and Chicago—emerged as the new centers of Ukrainian-American activity.

By this time, the Ukrainian-American community had developed a strong ethnic identity, as the Ukrainian Pavilion at the 1933 World's Fair in Chicago proved. Of the buildings at the fair representing national groups, the Ukrainian Pavilion was the only one that was not financed by a foreign government. Instead, donations from Ukrainian societies and individuals in both Europe and North America supported the project.

The Ukrainian Pavilion (left) at the 1933 World's Fair included a small stage, an open-air theater featuring Ukrainian dance ensembles and choirs, exhibits of Ukrainian folk art and history, and a Ukrainian restaurant (below).

Bombs destroyed an ancient church in Kiev during World War II.

Ruined by War

World War II (1939–1945) temporarily removed Ukraine from Soviet control when Germany invaded Ukraine in 1941. At first, Ukrainians naively believed that Adolf Hitler, Germany's dictator, would help them restore their independence. Many Ukrainians greeted the advancing German army as liberators. Within a few months, however, Hitler revealed his real purpose. Ukraine would be a permanent colony of Nazi Germany.

The first to feel the brunt of the Nazi occupation were Ukrainian Jews. German Nazis murdered no less than 850,000 Jews from Ukraine. The Nazis executed Ukrainian leaders by the thousands as well. According to Soviet estimates, the Nazis also sent about three million Ukrainians to Germany and Austria to work in factories and forced labor camps.

With the aid of American military supplies, the Soviet army drove the Germans out of Ukraine. By October 1944, Ukraine was back under Stalin's control. But Ukraine was in ruins. The conflict had destroyed more than 700 Ukrainian cities and 28,000 villages and had led to the death of some 6.8 million Ukrainian men, women, and children.

The terrible destruction of World War II brought great suffering to the people of Ukraine (above). A monument (left) now stands at Babyn Yar (Babi Yar), a ravine near Kiev where some 50,000 Ukrainians were executed by the Nazis. The vast majority, about 33,000, were Ukrainian Jews.

After the war, the UkSSR added northern Bukovina, eastern Galicia, and Carpatho-Ukraine to its republic. Stalin followed the same repressive policies against Ukrainian freedom in the newly acquired Ukrainian provinces. In 1946 the Soviets forced the independent Ukrainian Catholic Church in Galicia to join the Russian Orthodox Church. Stalin outlawed Catholicism and sent priests who refused to join the Soviet-controlled Russian church to Siberian labor camps.

Despite these harsh measures, Stalin insisted that the UkSSR was an independent state and should be a member of the newly formed United Nations (UN) in 1945. But the UkSSR's representatives to the UN did not act independently. Instead, they followed Moscow's direction and never once voted against the Communists.

Displaced Persons

Many Ukrainians left their homeland during World War II and refused to return while Ukraine was ruled by the Soviets. Such individuals, like other "displaced persons"

The United Ukrainian American Relief Committee helped this family come to America.

of the war, made up the third wave of Ukrainian immigration to the United States. The United States allowed these immigrants to enter the country under the Displaced Persons Act of 1948. Approximately 250,000 displaced persons of Ukrainian descent lived in Europe when this law was enacted. With assistance from a number of volunteer agencies, some 85,000 of these people found their way to the United States. The United Ukrainian-American Relief Committee, a charitable organization founded in 1944, had sponsored almost 33,000 Ukrainian immigrants by 1952. The National Catholic Welfare Conference also sponsored Ukrainian immigrants. After 1955 another 8,000 Ukrainians from Poland, Yugoslavia, western Europe, South America, and Australia migrated to North America.

A well-established Ukrainian-American community assisted new arrivals.

The third immigration to the United States differed from the earlier immigrations in a number of significant ways. For instance, most early Ukrainian immigrants, with the exception of the Protestants who were fleeing religious persecution, came to the United States to escape poverty. But the third immigration came to escape Soviet rule.

Almost 60 percent of the Ukrainians who came to the United States before 1914 were illiterate—they could not read or write. The Ukrainians who arrived during the second immigration rarely had more than five or six years of schooling. By contrast, most members of the third immigration had at least an eighth-grade education. Many were college graduates and professional people such as doctors, lawyers, and college professors.

Before World War II, most Ukrainians came from rural areas. A large percentage of the third immigration had lived in urban areas of Ukraine and could adjust more easily to American city life.

By the time the third immigration arrived, a well-established Ukrainian-American community could offer many kinds of assistance to the new arrivals. The first immigration had built the foundation of Ukrainian-American life, the second immigration strengthened it, and the third immigration reaped the benefits of a strong, well-knit community.

Independence for Ukraine

Conditions in Ukraine improved slightly following Stalin's death in 1953. At first, Nikita Khrushchev, the next Soviet leader, criticized Stalin's policies. Ukrainians increased their control of the Ukrainian Communist Party, and a new generation of young Ukrainian writers demanded a greater voice in their government.

Khrushchev's concessions allowed Ukrainians to renew their religious fervor, a development that caused Khrushchev to return to the antireligious policies of Stalin. Once again, the Soviets closed or destroyed churches and jailed religious leaders.

The Soviets could not stop the Ukrainian dissident movement, which was begun by a group of people who wrote and spoke out against the Soviet system. The writings of dissidents were smuggled to the West and published, leading to even more arrests by Soviet

On the day the Ukrainian parliament declared independence, Ukrainians held an anti-Communist rally in Kiev.

President Bill Clinton and President Leonid Kuchma, Ukraine's second president, on the south lawn of the White House during a formal welcoming ceremony in November 1994.

authorities. Despite repeated crackdowns, Ukrainians protested Soviet rule throughout the 1960s and 1970s.

Life in Ukraine changed dramatically once Soviet president Mikhail Gorbachev came to power in 1985 and introduced the policies of *glasnost* (openness) and *perestroika* (restructuring). Permitted more freedom, Ukrainians revived their traditions and pushed once again for independence.

Independence movements were also taking shape in other Soviet republics, forcing Gorbachev to propose self-government for the republics. A group of Soviets tried to take control and prevent such a change. The takeover attempt failed and Communist authority faltered. On August 24, 1991, the Ukrainian parliament declared Ukraine's independence. Over 90 percent of Ukrainians later approved this action in a national vote and elected Leonid Kravchuk, a former Communist Party official, president of the new Ukrainian state.

On December 25, 1991, Gorbachev resigned and the Soviet Union ceased to exist. For the first time since 1919, Ukraine was an independent nation. The blue and yellow flag of the Ukrainian National Republic quickly replaced the red and blue Soviet flag. The Ukrainian trident replaced the Soviet hammer and sickle.

3
THE UKRAINIAN EXPERIENCE IN AMERICA

The Ukrainians who came to the United States in the 19th century brought with them a strong desire to practice their religion in their new home. The church was the source of the Ukrainian national culture—their beliefs, folklore, and arts. For Ukrainian peasants especially, usually unable to read and therefore isolated from the Ukrainian literary revival of the 19th century, only one Ukrainian cultural institution existed—the church.

Other immigrants identified themselves by their homelands, calling themselves French Americans, Swedish Americans, and Irish Americans. But Ukrainian immigrants did not. Few Americans recognized the Ukrainian heritage because Ukraine had not existed as an independent nation for much of its history. Ukrainian immigrants believed that the establishment of a Ukrainian church in the United States would preserve their cultural identity.

Members of the Ukrainian-American club Soyuzivka pose for a reunion photo.

Carrying On the Traditions of Faith

Ukrainian-American Catholics found little religious satisfaction at other ethnic Catholic churches. Polish, Slovak, and Hungarian churches were Latin Rite, or Roman Catholic, churches. The Ukrainian Catholic Church, although united with Rome in 1596, was Byzantine Rite Catholic. Unlike Latin Rite Catholics, Ukrainian Catholics had a married clergy, attended only one kind of service, bowed and stood in church, and shunned the use of organs and statues.

The greatest obstacle to the immigrants' goal of establishing a Ukrainian Catholic Church was the power of the Latin Rite Catholic Church in the United States. Determined to include all American Catholics in one church, Latin Rite bishops opposed the formation of separate Catholic parishes, or districts of the church, based on the ethnic origins of parishioners. The bishops opposed efforts to start Ukrainian Catholic parishes, just as they opposed Polish, French, and German ones. Moreover, American Roman Catholic bishops would not accept the married clergy of the Ukrainian Catholic Church in their midst.

Some Ukrainian priests found that if they remained unmarried, they could avoid friction with American Catholic bishops. More clergy arrived from Ukraine and the Ukrainian Catholic Church in America grew. By 1898 there were 51 functioning Ukrainian Catholic churches or chapels in the United States.

Conflict between the Ukrainian Catholic clergy and American Roman Catholic bishops still continued. In 1889 Father Alexis Toth, a Catholic priest from Carpatho-Ukraine, presented himself to Bishop John Ireland of St. Paul, Minnesota, after assuming the position of pastor in Minneapolis. Despite the fact that Toth was a widower and could be considered unmarried, Bishop Ireland refused to acknowledge him. In 1891 Father Toth, still upset over the way Bishop Ireland had treated him, converted to the Russian Orthodox faith.

The power of the Roman Catholic Church in America was an obstacle to Ukrainian Catholic immigrants.

Father Toth persuaded other Rusyns to accept Russian Orthodoxy as the true faith of the people of Ukraine. "Neither the pope nor the American Catholic Church recognizes our unique status," Toth argued. "If we remain Catholics, we will lose our precious heritage." As a result, Toth's arguments convinced many immigrants to convert to the Russian Orthodox Church.

Alarmed by Toth's successes, Ukrainian Catholic priests in the United States and Europe pleaded with the Vatican, the government of the Roman Catholic Church, to appoint a Ukrainian bishop in the United States. Pope Pius X finally agreed, and in 1907, formally appointed Reverend Soter Ortynsky of Galicia as the first Ukrainian bishop in the United States. In 1913, Pope Pius X established a separate exarchate, or church province subject only to the pope, for Ukrainian Catholics. The pope placed Bishop Ortynsky and his successors on an equal level with other American bishops. By 1914 the Ukrainian exarchate included 206 parishes.

As leader of the Ukrainian-American Catholics, Bishop Ortynsky founded an orphanage, organized a fraternal insurance organization, planned a Ukrainian seminary,

An orphanage for girls founded by Bishop Ortynsky in Philadelphia

Most Reverend Soter Ortynsky **Reverend Constantine Bohachevsky**

and tried to unite the Ukrainian-American Catholic community.

In 1924 Bishop Constantine Bohachevsky succeeded Bishop Ortynsky as head of the Ukrainian Catholic Church in the United States. He directed the church toward a sound financial foundation with new church organizations and improvements to the Ukrainian school system. Bishop Bohachevsky championed the construction of school buildings for full-time elementary schools for Ukrainian children. The first such school opened in Philadelphia in 1925. By 1947 the church ran 18 Ukrainian day schools. In addition, most Ukrainian parishes conducted after-school and Saturday classes in Ukrainian culture. In the 1930s, the dynamic bishop also established a number of high schools and junior colleges.

Bishop Bohachevsky's work was not without controversy. In 1929 Pope Pius XI gave in to American Catholic pressure and prohibited marriage for all future

Students at St. George Ukrainian Catholic School (above) celebrate Taras Shevchenko Day. St. John the Baptist Ukrainian Catholic Church (left) in Hunter, New York, is an exact replica—down to the wooden nails—of a church in Carpatho-Ukraine.

Ukrainian Catholic priests in the United States. When the bishop decided to support and enforce the new ruling, some Ukrainian-American Catholic priests joined the newly established Ukrainian Orthodox Church, a Byzantine Rite church that allowed some priests to marry. Most Ukrainian Catholic priests remained loyal to Bishop Bohachevsky, however, and the Ukrainian Catholic Church survived and flourished.

With the exception of having a clergy that is now mostly celibate, the modern Ukrainian Church in America has preserved its ancient religious traditions. Currently, the Ukrainian Catholic Church is divided into one archeparchy (a large district of the church) headed by Metropolitan Stephen Sulyk, and three eparchies (smaller districts of the church) headed by bishops in Stamford, Connecticut; Parma, Ohio; and Chicago. In 1992, Ukrainian Catholic Church membership in the United States numbered about 145,000.

The heads of the Ukrainian Catholic Church in the United States (clockwise from upper-left): Metropolitan Stephen Sulyk (Archeparchy of Philadelphia); Bishop Basil Losten (Eparchy of Stamford); Bishop Robert Moskal (Eparchy of Parma); and Bishop Michael Wiwchar (Eparchy of Chicago)

Ukrainian Orthodoxy in the United States grew at a much slower pace than Ukrainian Catholicism. In the early part of the 20th century, a group of Ukrainians in Chicago established an independent Ukrainian People's Church. These Ukrainian Americans organized Ukrainian Orthodox parishes and proclaimed their unity with the Autocephalous Orthodox Church in Ukraine. In 1924 the All-Ukrainian Orthodox Council of Ukraine appointed Archbishop John Theodorovich to head the new church in America. By 1932 Archbishop Theodorovich's diocese included 32 parishes. The church that Theodorovich established is now the largest Ukrainian Orthodox congregation in the United States.

The congregation of the first Ukrainian church in Gorham, North Dakota, in the early 1900s

The leaders of the Ukrainian Orthodox Church of the U.S.A.: Metropolitan Constantine Bugan (left) and Bishop Anthony Scharba

Metropolitan Constantine Bugan heads the Ukrainian Orthodox Church of the U.S.A. with a 1992 membership totaling approximately 25,000.

The Ukrainian Protestant movement in the United States began in 1892. That year a group of Protestants, fleeing religious persecution in eastern Ukraine, founded one of the first Ukrainian farming communities near Yale, Virginia. Other groups of Protestant farmers settled in North Dakota, and by 1914, North Dakota had more Ukrainian agricultural communities than any other state.

Ukrainians established a Presbyterian parish in Newark, New Jersey, in 1909. Ukrainian Baptist congregations were established in Pennsylvania and Illinois by 1915. After 1950 Baptist congregations spread to Connecticut, Ohio, Minnesota, Wisconsin, Washington, and California. The largest Ukrainian Protestant church is the All-Ukrainian Evangelical Baptist Fellowship headed by the Reverend Volodymyr Domashovetz with a 1992 membership of 10,000.

Ukrainian children attending a Pennsylvania elementary school in 1902

Education for a Better Life

Since most Ukrainian immigrants arriving before 1914 were illiterate, they needed adult education classes to learn to read and write both English and Ukrainian. Ukrainian-American communities conducted most of these classes in libraries or reading rooms. Ukrainian Americans organized the first reading rooms in the late 1880s, and by 1920 most Ukrainian communities in America maintained at least one such center.

Ukrainian Americans established the first religious and cultural classes for their children in Shamokin, Pennsylvania, in 1893. By 1920, almost every Ukrainian-American locale held similar classes. Ukrainian children generally attended these classes for two hours, five evenings a week.

With the formation of the Ukrainian Teachers Society in 1913, Ukrainian youth education in the United States improved. The society developed an organized system of classes, published a teaching journal, and improved teaching methods through a series of conferences, seminars, and supervisory visits by master teachers. Ukrainian school enrollment rose rapidly between the two world wars (1918 to 1939).

The modern Ukrainian-American school system consists of day schools as well as Saturday heritage schools. In 1990 the Ukrainian Catholic Church operated 21 full-time elementary schools, 4 high schools, and 2 colleges. The Ukrainian Educational Council of the Ukrainian Congress Committee of America and the Ukrainian Orthodox Church run most heritage schools. Children attending heritage schools pursue an 11-year study program in Ukrainian language, history, geography, literature, and culture.

In 1968 the Ukrainian-American community created the Ukrainian Research Institute at Harvard University by establishing a fund to pay professors of Ukrainian history, literature, and language. In addition to offering doctoral degrees in Ukrainian studies, the institute publishes scholarly and historical works, offers summer courses, and houses a large collection of books on Ukraine.

Ukrainian books and artifacts can be found in museums in Chicago, Cleveland, Detroit, and New York City. The most extensive collection of Ukrainian archival materials is located at the Immigration History Research Center at the University of Minnesota.

The Ukrainian Research Institute, Harvard University

The Ukrainian-American Press Spreads the Word

The Ukrainian press in the United States began with Father Ahapius Honcharenko's *Alaska Herald* in 1868. The first Ukrainian-language newspaper in the United States was *Ameryka,* initially published by Father Wolansky in 1886.

The oldest continuously published Ukrainian-language newspaper in the world is *Svoboda,* which began publication in 1893. It was, in many respects, a union newspaper that supported the efforts of Ukrainian miners to improve their lives. Now published five days a week, *Svoboda* has been the official newspaper of the Ukrainian National Association since 1894.

By 1987 the Ukrainian press in America included some 69 Ukrainian-language periodicals, 23 bilingual publications, and 18 English-language publications. *The Ukrainian Weekly,* published by the Ukrainian National Association since 1933, is the most popular English-language Ukrainian publication in the United States.

Editors of The Ukrainian Weekly *view an upcoming edition of their publication.*

52

To Help Others, To Help Ourselves

The Ukrainian-American community formed strong, self-sustaining organizations that provided a variety of cultural, financial, political, scientific, and recreational programs. These organizations have helped Ukrainians adjust to American life.

Fraternal insurance associations have two main purposes. They provide life insurance for their members and lend financial support to various Ukrainian enterprises in both the United States and Canada. The first such association in the United States was Father Wolansky's Brotherhood of St. Nicholas.

There are four Ukrainian fraternal organizations in existence today. These organizations support Ukrainian

Members of the first Brotherhood of St. Nicholas, 1885

churches, provide scholarships, and publish books, newspapers, and magazines. The Ukrainian National Association, founded in 1894, is the largest of the Ukrainian fraternal insurance associations. The three other associations are the Ukrainian Fraternal Association, the Providence Association of Ukrainian Catholics, and the Ukrainian National Aid Association.

Beginning in 1947, Ukrainian credit unions were established in cities throughout the United States. Since then, they have experienced continuous growth and success. Today there are 28 Ukrainian-American credit unions, with assets approaching one billion dollars. These credit unions are working to establish similar institutions in independent Ukraine.

Ukrainian immigrants wanted to be patriotic Americans, sensitive to the needs of their adopted country. They created a number of citizens' clubs during the early days of the Ukrainian immigration. These clubs prepared immigrants for citizenship and taught them the principles of American democracy. The Ukrainian National Association used its newspaper, *Svoboda*, for this purpose before World War I. The association urged its members to become American citizens, to participate actively in American civic and political organizations, and to follow the examples of great American patriots in their everyday lives. *Svoboda's* pages contained frequent discussions of the American Revolution and the rights guaranteed by the U.S. Constitution.

Ukrainians played an important role in the early days of the U.S. labor movement. Several Ukrainian-American leaders followed the work of Father Wolansky in advocating unions. Ukrainian clergy stood firmly behind their parishioners' union demands for better pay and working conditions. During an especially long strike in 1900, Father Konstankevych of Shamokin, Pennsylvania, offered to mortgage the Ukrainian church to provide funds for striking miners. Through the efforts of the Ukrainians and other Slavs, the miners finally organized a strong and effective United Mine Workers Union.

Ukrainian-American labor unions tried to better the lives of immigrant coal miners.

Ukrainian Americans formed most of their political groups to support the restoration of an independent Ukraine. Before World War I, the Ukrainian fraternal insurance associations usually initiated this work. Between the two world wars, Ukrainian Americans established two political organizations, the Hetman Association (Sich) and the Organization for the Rebirth of Ukraine (ODWU). Both national organizations had branches in most Ukrainian-American communities and held adult education classes, seminars, and concerts as a part of their activities.

Members of the third immigration (those arriving after World War II) formed a number of Ukrainian political organizations. The largest and most active of these have been the Organization for the Defense of Four Freedoms in Ukraine (OOCHSU) and the Democratic Organization of Ukrainians Formerly Persecuted by the Soviet Government (DOBRUS). All Ukrainian-American political organizations are involved in rebuilding independent Ukraine.

Two youth organizations, Sokil and Sich, originated in 1902 as athletic clubs for young Ukrainian-American men. The Hetman Association founded a branch for young men in the 1920s. The Organization for the Rebirth of Ukraine organized the Young Ukrainian Nationalists (MUN) in 1933 to publicize Ukraine's freedom crusade.

The most active youth organizations have been the Ukrainian Youth Association of America (SUMA), the Ukrainian scouting organization known as Plast, and the Organization of Democratic Ukrainian Youth (ODUM), all of which were founded between 1948 and 1950 for the purpose of preserving the Ukrainian heritage. All three own and operate summer camps in New York and the Midwest.

Ukrainian students attending American universities organized the Federation of Ukrainian Student Organizations of America (SUSTA) in 1953. SUSTA started a fund in 1957 and contributed more than a million dollars to support the Ukrainian Research Institute at Harvard University.

Ukrainian-American students raised money for the Ukrainian Research Institute at Harvard University.

The first Ukrainian women's organization, the Sisterhood of St. Olga, was founded in 1897 but no longer exists. The largest surviving women's organization, the Ukrainian National Women's League of America (UNWLA), was established in 1925. UNWLA members participate in a variety of community projects, such as raising funds for Ukrainian churches and schools, helping needy Ukrainians, sponsoring cultural events and exhibits, and preparing a course of study for preschool Ukrainian children.

Another active women's organization is the Ukrainian Gold Cross, first organized in 1931. This organization raises funds for needy Ukrainians and sponsors cultural activities, children's camps, and preschool centers.

In keeping with their interest in scholarship, members of the third immigration organized American branches of the Shevchenko Scientific Society and the Ukrainian Academy of Sciences after World War II. Both societies

In 1922 Ukrainian-American women picketed the White House to protest Polish rule of Ukraine.

have researched and published extensively in both the Ukrainian and English languages. Two new academic societies, the V.K. Lypynsky East European Research Institute and the Ukrainian Historical Society publish materials on Ukrainian history.

In addition to the scientific societies, Ukrainian doctors, engineers, teachers, and other professionals have established their own societies. The highly active Ukrainian Medical Society publishes a medical journal and offers scholarships. In 1990 it became the first Ukrainian-American professional society to hold its annual convention in Ukraine.

The Ukrainian-American community combined its organizational strength by forming a nationwide union of organizations. The Ukrainian National Council, established in 1915, was reorganized into the United Ukrainian Organizations (Obyednenya) in the early

A 1934 aviation club of the Organization for the Rebirth of Ukraine

1920s. And in 1940, this organization became the Ukrainian Congress Committee of America (UCCA).

On July 17, 1959, the UCCA was instrumental in the passage of U.S. Congress Public Law 86–90 mandating an annual observance of Captive Nations Week. For years, this observance reminded Americans of all nations suffering under Communist oppression. Recognizing the right of 22 peoples, including the Ukrainians, to national self-rule, Congress passed the resolution that "the people of the United States share with them their aspirations for the recovery of their freedom and independence." The third week of July was designated as Captive Nations Week.

Following a turbulent convention in 1980, a number of organizations left the UCCA. In 1983 some of them formed the Ukrainian American Coordinating Council (UACC). Other organizations decided to remain neutral, avoiding involvement with either national federation.

Like other immigrants, Ukrainians who came to the United States had to adjust to a new country, a strange language, and unfamiliar customs. As they adapted to their new lives, Ukrainian Americans drew comfort and support from their common heritage. Their churches—an important part of life in their native Ukraine—provided a sense of community. Organizations, schools, and newspapers helped new immigrants adjust to American life. These institutions linked Ukrainian Americans to their eastern European roots and encouraged individual contributions to American society.

4
CONTRIBUTIONS TO
AMERICAN LIFE

St. Nicholas Ukrainian Catholic Cathedral, located in Chicago

Architecture

The Ukrainian church, traditionally the center of Ukrainian community life, has contributed to the architectural variety of the United States. Hundreds of Ukrainian churches with their many domes can be found throughout the United States, especially in northeastern Pennsylvania and sections of North Dakota. Most of these churches were built prior to 1920.

Early Ukrainian immigrants made every effort to preserve the architectural style of Ukraine in the churches they built in the United States. St. Nicholas Ukrainian Catholic Cathedral in Chicago, Illinois, is a magnificent example. Completed in 1914, St. Nicholas has 13 domes and seats 1,200 people. Nine Byzantine-style paintings, reproductions of mosaic art found in St. Sophia's Church in Kiev, decorate the church. Ukrainian artist and priest Father Hlib Verchovsky planned and drew the sketches for the window ornamentations and altars. Another Ukrainian, Bohdan Katamay, created the paintings and most of the decoration.

The Dance, *a sculpture
(left) by Alexander
Archipenko (below)*

Fine Arts

Alexander Archipenko, a sculptor, was possibly the greatest Ukrainian-American artist. Born in Kiev in 1887, Archipenko attended the Kiev Art Academy and had his first solo show at the age of 19. Moving to Paris in 1908, he studied art at the École des Beaux-Arts. Archipenko came to the United States in 1923 and became an American citizen in 1928. He taught art at universities across the country, and by 1962, had 119 solo exhibitions. Archipenko's works can be found in major art museums throughout the world.

Throughout his career, Archipenko searched for new modes of expression. Rejecting realistic (true-to-life) styles of sculpture, Archipenko studied the paintings of Pablo Picasso and Georges Braque. These artists experimented with cubism, a style of painting that breaks apart and emphasizes an object's shape and surfaces. In 1913 Archipenko created his famous *Boxers,* recognized as the first cubist sculpture.

In addition to pioneering cubist sculpture, Archipenko introduced "sculpto-painting," in which he attached separate parts of a figure to a flat surface before painting the entire piece. Archipenko also experimented with "spatial sculpture." He created open shapes within his sculpture. In this approach, the material framed the space, giving space itself a new importance.

Another acclaimed Ukrainian-American artist was Jacques Hnizdovsky, described by art critics as "a painter of the invisible" and a master of "visual poetry." Hnizdovsky, who specialized in woodcut prints, exhibited his work throughout the world. His art can be found in museums in Philadelphia, Boston, and Cleveland, as well as in various private collections.

Two prints by Jacques Hnizdovsky, **The Cat** *(below) and* **Pine Tree** *(right)*

Folk Arts and Music

The man most responsible for popularizing Ukrainian folk dance in America was Vasile Avramenko. He came to the United States in 1928 and eventually organized more than 100 Ukrainian dance groups throughout North America. In 1931, some 300 Avramenko-trained Ukrainian dancers performed at the Metropolitan Opera House in New York. Later, Avramenko dance groups appeared at the Civic Opera House in Chicago and performed for Eleanor Roosevelt on the White House lawn. Avramenko's pupils and others continue his work throughout the United States.

Vasile Avramenko

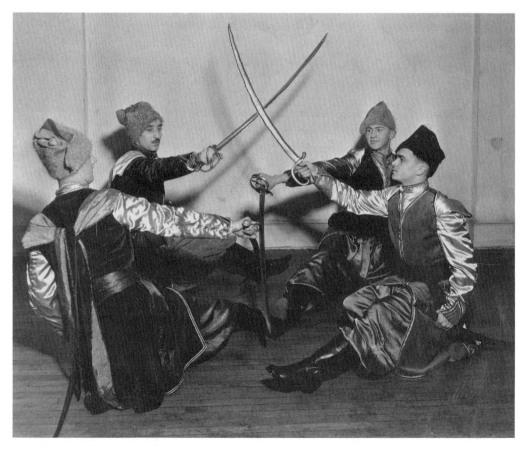

A Ukrainian-American dance troupe performs a traditional sword dance.

Thousands of Ukrainian-American women practice embroidery, a folk art used extensively in the Ukrainian church and in traditional dress. Some of the best examples of Ukrainian embroidery can be found in the work of Oksana Tkachuk, an expert in the *nyzynka* stitch—a technique popular in Carpatho-Ukraine. Her work includes hundreds of embroidered scarves, blouses, doilies, pillowcases, curtains, and drapes.

Ukrainian-American women also practice the popular art of Easter-egg painting, which dates back to ancient Kievan times. The Ukrainian Easter egg, or *pysanka,* is famous for its delicate and intricate beauty. While hundreds of Ukrainian women practice this tradition in their homes each year, a few are recognized as masters of the art. Maria Procai of Minneapolis is one of the many artists responsible for popularizing Ukrainian Easter-egg painting in the United States.

Ukrainian Americans continue to practice these traditional arts (clockwise from below): Pysanka, hand-painted Easter eggs; wood carving; and embroidery

An old Ukrainian saying states "When two Ukrainians meet, we have the beginning of another choir." For Ukrainians, song is a second language. In 1887 Volodymyr Simenovych organized the first Ukrainian choir in North America in Shenandoah, Pennsylvania. From then on, each Ukrainian community established its own church choir almost as soon as the community was organized. Early choirs sang only during church services, but gradually they included folk songs. A number of choirs have produced their own musicals.

The United States came to know Ukrainian music with the arrival of the Ukrainian National Chorus, which was formed in the days of the Ukrainian National Republic. Directed by Professor Alexander Koshetz, the chorus toured Europe and the United States in 1922 and 1923 to popular acclaim. Soon Witmark Educational Publishers began printing Ukrainian songs in English. The Ukrainian National Chorus introduced the beautiful "Carol of the Bells" by Nicholas Leontovych to American audiences. The song is now an American Christmas classic.

Alexander Koshetz (in tan overcoat, holding hat) is welcomed in New York City with bread and salt, the traditional Ukrainian greeting to newcomers.

After the Ukrainian National Republic fell to Soviet rule, Koshetz and his entire chorus remained in the United States. Many former chorus members gained musical fame on their own. Leo Sorochinsky led the Chicago Ukrainian Chorus in two Chicagoland Music Festivals. Competing against top choirs from all over the Midwest, the choir won first and second place honors every year from 1930 to 1934.

The Taras Shevchenko Ukrainian Bandurist Chorus of Detroit is an accomplished Ukrainian male vocal ensemble, originally established in Ukraine in 1923 and reorganized in the United States in 1949. Most of the singers in this unusual musical group accompany themselves on the *bandura,* the Ukrainian national instrument. Resembling a combination of the lute and the harp, the bandura has 30 to 60 strings and a range of five octaves. Following annual tours of North America, the Bandurist Chorus returned to Ukraine in 1991, where they enjoyed a triumphant tour through 14 cities.

Individual Ukrainian musicians have excelled in their American careers. Metropolitan Opera star Paul Plishka has appeared in more than 40 roles. Andrij Dobriansky has been a member of the Met since 1969.

The Taras Shevchenko Ukrainian Bandurist Chorus of Detroit

Nick Adams (far left) in his TV series The Rebel and Anna Sten (above)

Entertainment

Many Ukrainians have achieved recognition in American motion pictures. Anna Sten, the first successful Ukrainian actor in Hollywood, appeared in a number of films during the 1930s. John Hodiak, another Hollywood actor of Ukrainian descent, starred with Tallulah Bankhead in *Lifeboat* in 1942. Later he appeared in a variety of movie hits, from the musical *The Harvey Girls* to the war film *A Bell for Adano*. Just before his death in 1955, he appeared on the Broadway stage in *The Caine Mutiny Court Martial*.

Even when he was very young, Nick Adams (born Nicholas Adamchok in Nanticoke, Pennsylvania) wanted to be nothing else but a Hollywood star. After hitchhiking to Hollywood, he received his first break in the James Dean movie *Rebel Without a Cause*. Later he appeared with Andy Griffith in *No Time for Sergeants*. Just before his death, he starred in his own television series, *The Rebel*.

John Hodiak

Measuring 6 feet, 6 inches tall and weighing 245 pounds, the biggest Ukrainian in Hollywood was Mike Mazurki. Born in Lviv, Mazurki came to America at the age of 6. Invariably cast as a villain or a comic heavy, Mazurki was actually a mild-mannered person and a graduate of Manhattan College who spoke four languages and played the violin. He appeared in more than 125 films, including *Donovan's Reef, It's a Mad Mad Mad Mad World,* and *Cheyenne Autumn.*

Jack Palance was born Walter Jack Palahniuk in 1921 in Lattimer Mines, Pennsylvania. Palance has acted in stage plays, motion pictures, and television movies. He was nominated for an Oscar as best supporting actor in *Sudden Fear* (1952) and *Shane* (1953). He finally won an Oscar in 1992 for his comic portrayal of a rugged cowboy in *City Slickers.*

Jack Palance (left) played Curly in City Slickers. *Mike Mazurki (below, holding knife) often portrayed comic villains.*

A rising Ukrainian-American film star is George Dzundza, an actor with Broadway experience and film credits ranging from *The Deer Hunter* to *The Butcher's Wife*. He also starred in the television series *Law and Order*.

George Dzundza

Politics

During the 1890s, Ukrainians became active in Ukrainian affiliates of the Democratic and Republican parties.

Ukrainian-born Dr. Nikolai Rusel (originally named Sudzilovsky), arrived in San Francisco in the early 1880s and practiced medicine there until 1895. He worked closely with Ukrainian-American publisher Father Honcharenko in the creation of a pan-Slavic society and shared many of the Orthodox priest's ideals. Later Dr. Rusel moved to Hawaii, where in 1896 he helped organize the Hawaiian Medical Society. When the islands became a territory of the United States, he became a leader of the Independent Home Rule Party, which gained a majority in the first territorial senate. In 1901 Dr. Rusel was elected to this senate and became its presiding officer. While in office, he supported public health improvements, the banning of alcoholic beverages, better public schools, the establishment of local libraries, more universities, and voting rights for women.

Although he was never able to realize all of his plans for Hawaii, Dr. Rusel helped pass a law that allowed landless families to obtain land. This law benefited 365 Ukrainian immigrants who obtained land on the island of Hawaii.

Ukrainians have served in the state legislatures of Hawaii, Indiana, Illinois, Michigan, New Jersey, New York, Pennsylvania, and Rhode Island.

Ukrainian Americans have also served in appointed government positions. Joseph Charyk, president of the Communications Satellite Corporation, was Air Force undersecretary (assistant to the secretary) from 1960 to 1963. Dr. Michael Yarymovych served as the deputy director of the Energy Research Development Agency (ERDA) during President Gerald Ford's administration. Dr. Myron B. Kuropas has served in the Ford White House as the special assistant to the president for ethnic affairs. President Ronald Reagan appointed Dr. Lev Dobriansky U.S. ambassador to the Bahamas, and President George Bush appointed Roman Popadiuk as U.S. ambassador to Ukraine.

On local levels, Ukrainians have served as mayors and members of city councils and school boards. One of the best known political figures among Ukrainians is Mary Beck, who served on the Detroit City Council from 1950 to 1970. She was the first Ukrainian-American woman elected to public office and served in office longer than any other Ukrainian American.

Illinois Republican State Senator Walter Dudycz is a Ukrainian American.

Mary Beck

Education and Research

Leading the list of prominent Ukrainians in scientific research is Igor Sikorsky, a native of Kiev. In 1913 Sikorsky built and flew the first successful multimotored aircraft. He came to the United States in 1919 and founded the Sikorsky Aviation Corporation. Sikorsky invented a number of aircraft, including "flying boats" and the first successful long-range airplanes known as clippers. In fact, the Sikorsky clippers pioneered transoceanic travel. In 1939 Sikorsky developed the first successful helicopter in the West, and set a world's record for sustained helicopter flying in 1941. Sikorsky is recognized as one of the creators of the modern helicopter.

Dr. George Kistiakowsky came to the United States from Kiev in 1926. A member of the National Academy of Sciences, Kistiakowsky taught chemistry at Harvard University from 1930 to 1960. In 1960 he served as

Igor Sikorsky

Sikorsky built this forerunner of the modern helicopter.

President Dwight Eisenhower's chief science adviser.

Many Ukrainian-American scholars have specialized in Ukrainian and Slavic studies. Dr. George Vernadsky, the most prominent Ukrainian in the social sciences, came to the United States in 1927. Before joining the history faculty at Yale, Vernadsky taught at Stanford, Columbia, and Johns Hopkins Universities. He contributed greatly to Russian studies and wrote many scholarly works on the subject.

Military Service

Ukrainians have served the United States in all of the country's wars, and many have been decorated for bravery in action. During World War II, Nicholas Minue of Carteret, New Jersey, was the sole attacker of a German machine gun installation in Tunisia. Minue completely destroyed a German position and continued to fight until he was fatally wounded. For this act of bravery, he won the Congressional Medal of Honor.

Lieutenant Colonel Theodore Kalakuka became the first Ukrainian graduate of West Point. Assigned to the Philippines, Kalakuka personally saved a wounded soldier during a Japanese air attack. He risked his life during another air raid to save valuable medical supplies and lead an attack on a Japanese landing party after the American company commander was wounded. Captured by the Japanese, Kalakuka died of malaria in a prison camp. After his death, he was awarded the Silver Star and two oak leaf clusters.

Ukrainian Americans, some of whom had recently arrived under the 1948 Displaced Persons Act, served in the Korean War. Many of them died fighting for their adopted homeland. Hundreds of Ukrainian Americans also fought and died in the Vietnam War. General Samuel Jaskilka served in the U.S. Marines during World War II, the Korean War (during which he was twice awarded the Silver Star for heroism), and the Vietnam War. A one-time assistant commandant of the Marine Corps, he retired a four-star general.

General Samuel Jaskilka

71

(From left), Zenon Snylyk, George Andrie, and Walter Tkaczuk

Sports

Ukrainian Americans have excelled at many sports, especially soccer, hockey, and football.

Two Ukrainian soccer teams have reached the United States national soccer championships. The Ukrainian Nationals of Philadelphia were the champions in 1961, 1962, 1964, and 1966. The New York Ukrainians captured the U.S. crown in 1965. Zenon Snylyk holds the national record for his selection to three consecutive U.S. Olympic soccer teams, in 1956, 1960, and 1964.

Bill Moseienko played hockey for the Chicago Blackhawks and holds a record for scoring three goals in 21 seconds. New York Rangers goaltender Terry Sawchuk set a record for 103 shut-outs. While playing for the New York Rangers during the 1969-1970 season, Dave Balon and Walter Tkaczuk were part of the National Hockey League's highest scoring line.

Bronko Nagurski, who played professional football in the 1930s, is remembered as one of the greatest fullbacks ever. George Andrie, a defensive end for the Dallas Cowboys, was also a football standout. Other Ukrainian Americans who played pro football include Bill Malinchak, George Tatasovic, John Machuzak, and Don Chuy.

Ukrainian Olympic skaters Viktor Petrenko and Oksana Baiul live and train in the United States.

Mike Ditka

The most prominent Ukrainian American in football is Mike Ditka, former coach of the Chicago Bears. Born in Aliquippa, Pennsylvania, "Iron Mike" began his professional football career with the Chicago Bears in 1961 as a tight end and was named Rookie of the Year. Ditka was a key player during the Bears' 1963 championship season and caught a record 75 passes in 1964. After leaving the Bears in 1966, he was with the Philadelphia Eagles and the Dallas Cowboys, playing in the 1971 and 1972 Super Bowls. He retired as a player in 1973 but remained with the Cowboys as an assistant coach. In 1981 Ditka was hired as head coach by his old team, the Chicago Bears. When the Bears won the Super Bowl in 1986, Ditka was named NFL Coach of the Year. He was inducted into the NFL Hall of Fame two years later.

Ukrainian-American Dr. Anatol Lysyj with a parade banner that reads "We won't let Ukraine be sold"

If there is a motto to guide the Ukrainian community in America, it is one by Ukraine's poet, Taras Shevchenko: "Absorb all cultures but forget not your own." As one of America's best-organized ethnic groups, Ukrainians have not forgotten their heritage after more than a century in the United States. For decades Ukrainian Americans have celebrated Ukrainian Independence Day on January 22 and Taras Shevchenko Day on March 14 in the undying belief that someday Ukraine would be a free and independent nation once again. What seemed like an impossible dream is a reality—Ukraine is finally on the world's map. American-born Ukrainians now travel back to Ukraine to help rebuild a nation devastated by 70 years of Communist oppression. Hundreds of Ukrainian-American doctors, lawyers, engineers, architects, teachers, college professors, businesspersons, and others—all fluent in the Ukrainian language because their parents would not let them "forget their own" — are in Ukraine today. They have gone to guide Ukraine's new leaders to create the kind of democratic, entrepreneurial society Ukrainian Americans have enjoyed for so many years. This payback will benefit both Ukraine and the United States.

GLOSSARY

ataman: a Cossack commander

brotherhood: an association organized for a specific purpose, such as the Brotherhood of St. Nicholas. This brotherhood was the first Ukrainian-American burial society.

burial society: a group organized to provide loans and money for funeral expenses. In the United States, fraternal insurance associations have provided these services to the Ukrainian-American community.

Byzantine Rite: one of the 21 rites within the universal Catholic Church of which the Roman Rite, sometimes called the Latin Rite, is the largest. All of the rites recognize the primacy of the pope in Rome. The Ukrainian Catholic Church is a Byzantine Rite church.

collectives: businesses or farms owned and run by the government

Communism: an economic and political system based on government ownership and control of all land, factories, economic resources, and consumer goods. The Russian party of Communists that led the 1917 revolution were called Bolsheviks.

Cossacks: a military order formed of Ukrainian and Russian frontier settlers that developed in the 1500s

czar: the title of the ruler of the Russian Empire until the 1917 revolution

democracy: a system of government by the people in which every person has an equal vote

exarchate: a district of the Ukrainian Catholic Church led by a bishop who is subject only to the pope

hammer and sickle: the national symbol of the former Union of Soviet Socialist Republics (USSR)

hetman: the commander in chief of the Cossacks; also, the title given to the Ukrainian leader who was appointed by landowners after the Rada was overthrown in 1918

Metropolitan See: a province of the Eastern Christian Church overseen by an archbishop, or Metropolitan

Polonization: a Polish governmental policy that attempted to replace the traditions and institutions of Ukraine with Polish traditions and institutions

rada: the ruling assembly of the Cossacks. The ruling assembly of the Ukrainian National Republic was named the Rada.

republic: a system of government, such as the U.S. government, with an elected president and an assembly of elected representatives of the people

Russification: a Russian governmental policy that attempted to replace the traditions and institutions of Ukraine and other subject countries with Russian traditions and institutions

sich: fortress or community of the Cossacks

trident: a three-pronged spear. The trident is the national symbol of Ukraine.

INDEX

Groups featured in Lerner's In America series:

AMERICAN INDIANS	JEWS
CUBANS	KOREANS
DANES	LEBANESE
FILIPINOS	MEXICANS
FRENCH	NORWEGIANS
GERMANS	PUERTO RICANS
GREEKS	SCOTS &
IRISH	SCOTCH-IRISH
ITALIANS	UKRAINIANS
JAPANESE	VIETNAMESE

About the Author

Myron B. Kuropas, a Ukrainian American, graduated from Loyola University and earned his M.A. at Chicago's Roosevelt University. He received his Ph.D. at the University of Chicago, where he wrote his dissertation on the Ukrainian immigration. In 1991, the University of Toronto Press published his book *The Ukrainian-Americans: Roots and Aspirations*. Dr. Kuropas has pursued a distinguished career in both government and education and is presently an adjunct professor in the Department of Leadership and Educational Policy Studies at Northern Illinois University. Dr. Kuropas makes his home in DeKalb, Illinois, with his wife, Alexandra. They have two married sons, Stephen and Michael.

ACKNOWLEDGMENTS: Photos and illustrations used with permission of Bohdan A. Lysyj, p. 2; *The Ukrainian Weekly,* pp. 6, 28, 29 (both), 41, 42, 52, 59, 71, 72 (left); Jeff Greenberg, pp. 7, 32 (bottom); IPS, 8, 12 (top), 13, 23; Laura Westlund, pp. 9, 15, 30, 75, 76; *Kiev,* p. 10; Culver Pictures, Inc., p. 11 (top); TASS from SOVFOTO, p. 11 (bottom); Ukrainian National Museum, Chicago, IL, pp. 12 (center right), 20, 21, 35 (top), 63 (top and bottom left); Cherokee Book Shop, p. 14; League of Americans of Ukrainian Descent, courtesy, Walter Nechay, p. 18; *Forum,* p. 19; Immigration History Research Center, University of Minnesota, pp. 22, 38, 48, 64; The New York Public Library, Astor, Lenox and Tilden Foundations, p. 24; Dr. Wasyl Halich, p. 25 (top); Library of Congress, p. 25 (bottom); Ukrainian Diocesan Museum and Library, Stamford, CT, p. 26 (left); National Archives, pp. 31, 37 (top); drawing by Mykhailo Ivanchenko, courtesy, Bohdan Hodiak, p. 32 (top); Bohdan Hodiak, pp. 33, 37 (bottom); Minnesota Historical Society Archives, p. 34; Reuters / Bettmann, p. 40; Ukrainian National Women's League, p. 46 (top); Dr. Myron Kuropas, pp. 47 (top right and left, bottom right), 49 (both); © Andrew Ulicki, courtesy, Bishop Michael Wiwchar, p. 47 (bottom left); Ukrainian Research Institute, Harvard University, p. 51; The Ukrainian Academy of Arts and Sciences, pp. 60 (both), 61 (both), 62 (top right); Kenneth M. Wright, Minnesota Historical Society, p. 62 (bottom); Dr. Antol and Mrs. Daria Lysyj, pp. 63 (right), 74; Hollywood Book and Poster, pp. 66 (top left and right), 67 (both), 68; 20th Century Fox, p. 66 (bottom); Office of the Senator, Walter W. Dudycz, p. 69 (top right); Burton Historical Collection, Detroit Public Library, p. 69 (bottom); Sikorsky Aircraft, p. 70 (both); Dallas Cowboys, p. 72 (center); New York Rangers, p. 72 (right); Lois Elfman, p. 73 (top); Chicago Bears, p. 73 (bottom).

Photos used with permission of The Ukrainian Museum, New York, NY: pp. 35 (bottom), 36, 46 (bottom); donated by Roman Iwasiwka, p. 16; donated by Johanna Luciow, Minneapolis, MN, p. 17; courtesy of Olga Dudish, Shenandoah, PA, p. 26 (right); courtesy of Ukrainian Diocesan Museum and Library, Stamford, CT, pp. 44, 45 (right), 53, 54, 56, 57; donated by Msgr. Basil Feddish, Willimantic, CT, p. 45 (left); donated by Bavolack-Yonkovig-Pronchick Families, King of Prussia, PA, p. 50; donated by Rozalia Fenchynsky, New York, NY, p. 65.

Front cover by Nancy Smedstad / IPS. Back cover by Festival of Nations.